A Family in Hungary

A pronunciation guide for the Hungarian names and words used in this book appears on page 28.

Map on pages 4-5 by J. Michael Roy. Photographs on page 8, top, and page 11 by Adrian Harvey.

LIBRARY OF CONGRESS CATALOGING-IN-PUBLICATION DATA

St. John, Jetty.
 A family in Hungary.

 Summary: Describes the home, customs, work, school, and amusements of two Hungarian sisters and their family living in Budapest.
 1. Hungary—Social life and customs—Juvenile literature. [1. Family life—Hungary. 2. Hungary—Social life and customs] I. Harvey, Nigel, ill. II. Title.
 DB920.5.S77   1988   943.9   87-33936
 ISBN 0-8225-1683-7 (lib. bdg.)

Manufactured in the United States of America

1 2 3 4 5 6 7 8 9 10 98 97 96 95 94 93 92 91 90 89 88

A Family in Hungary

Jetty St. John

Photographs by Nigel Harvey

Lerner Publications Company • Minneapolis

Anna (right), 12, and Zsuzsa (whose nickname is Suzi), 10, are sisters. They live in Budapest, which is the capital of Hungary. Hungary is in Eastern Europe and is surrounded by five other countries. It takes Anna and Suzi ten minutes by streetcar to get from their house down to the Danube River.

This large river flows between the hills of Buda on the west and the plains of Pest in the east. Buda and Pest are twin cities joined by a number of bridges.

Over a thousand years ago, tribes of horsemen called Magyars rode into Hungary from the mountains of Asia and settled in Hungary. Most Hungarians today are descendants of the Magyars. The word "Magyar" means Hungarian.

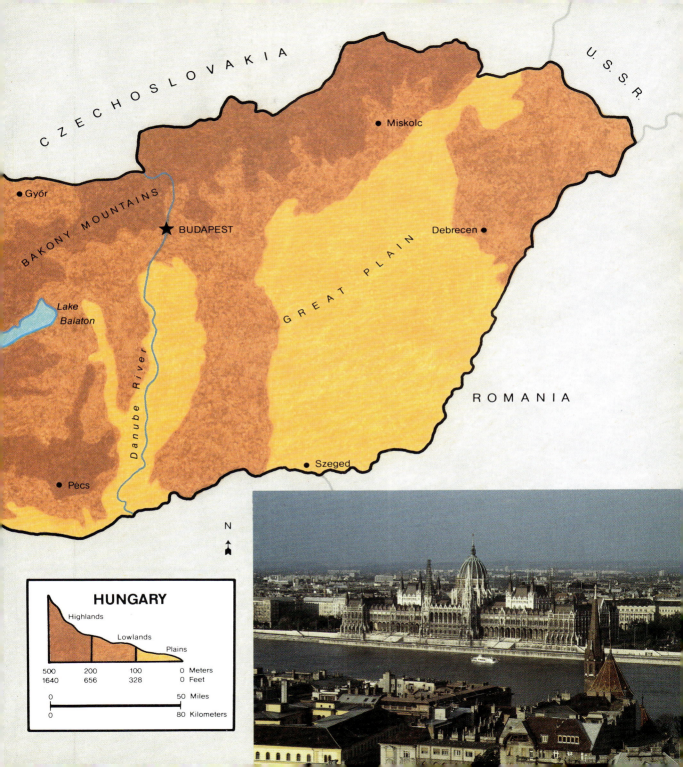

CZECHOSLOVAKIA

U.S.S.R.

• Győr

• Miskolc

BAKONY MOUNTAINS

★ BUDAPEST

Debrecen •

Lake Balaton

G R E A T   P L A I N

Danube River

R O M A N I A

• Pécs

• Szeged

N

HUNGARY

Highlands

Lowlands

Plains

500	200	100	0 Meters
1640	656	328	0 Feet

0		50 Miles
0		80 Kilometers

The girls' mother writes books about Hungarian folklore. She has a collection of national costumes that are family heirlooms. Some of the outfits are over 100 years old, and she keeps them in a chest with special powder and layers of paper to protect them from bugs.

Dr. Szegedy-Maszák, the girls' father, is a well-known professor of literature at the University of Budapest. He also teaches at the Academy of Fine Arts. Many Hungarians work at two jobs so they'll have enough money for food and clothes. Foreign universities sometimes ask Anna's father to come and teach Hungarian literature. The girls visited the United States with their parents and they learned to speak English there.

Anna and Suzi also have an older brother, Zoltán, but he is away from home doing his military service before he goes to college. At age 18, Hungarian boys must serve 18 months in the military.

The family lives in the northwest part of the city, where there are hills with many trees. Their house once belonged to Dr. Szegedy-Maszák's parents, but about 30 years ago the government divided it and gave the top half to people who supported the government.

During school vacations Suzi and Anna sometimes ride in to work with their mother in the family car. Her office is nestled in the castle walls of the old part of Buda.

The castle inside the walls was bombed during World War II, but it has been rebuilt. Down the side streets, some of the buildings are more than 800 years old. The ramparts of the city walls are fun to explore, and Suzi and Anna have been in a section of the city dungeons.

In the courtyard, tourists can buy handmade pottery, paintings, and embroidered goods. The cost of most items is set by the government, so people pay the same price everywhere they shop. Suzi and Anna often see violinists playing at people's tables in the restaurants. The girls buy ice cream from a stall before returning to their mother's office.

Many children go on trips with the Young Pioneers, a youth organization sponsored by the government. All over Hungary, children belong to Young Pioneers. Anna is the leader of her branch, which is called the Road Breakers. She wears a red scarf. Suzi is a Little Drummer and wears a blue scarf. The girls meet with their groups once a week.

The groups have paper drives, help old people with their shopping, and take classes on how to be good citizens. Once a year there is a ceremony at school in which the leader of an outstanding group ties a ribbon onto a pole in the center of the building. Anna put on a ribbon this year. Most children in Anna's school belong to the Young Pioneers, and each student must go on at least three day trips a year.

Summer vacation is from June to September. The sun shines then and the temperature is around 70° F (21° C). When it is this warm, children wear jeans and T-shirts. At school they pull a *köpeny*, or smock, over their every-day clothes. During the Christmas and Easter vacations it can get below freezing, and in December it often snows.

Children go to school from the ages of 6 to 16. Then they learn a trade or continue their studies until they go to college. At age 11, all Hungarian children learn Russian. Anna is good at languages, but her favorite subject is Hungarian literature.

After school, Anna and Suzi take rhythmic gymnastics lessons. They learn many routines, sometimes using ribbons and umbrellas. When the children get home from school, Bundás, their *puli*, or Hungarian sheepdog, plays with them in the yard. Dr. Szegedy-Maszák often works in the yard in the fresh air. One day he looked up from his books to find he was surrounded by a herd of wild boars which had strayed down from the hills. Since then he has put up a fence to keep out the intruders.

The family enjoys spending time in the yard. Their 150-year-old acacia tree provides shade, and Anna and Suzi think it's fun to climb. When the family's house was divided in two, half of the yard was given to the people upstairs. These people say that the old tree must also be shared, since they do not own a tree as large.

Anna's father plays the piano. When he was a student he started training as a concert pianist, but his hands were damaged in an accident. He now teaches the girls to play. Anna practices while her mother cooks the evening meal.

On weekends the girls help with the cooking. A special dish they make is called paprika chicken. Their mother buys special peppers to add to the dish, and the meal is served with salad and noodles. Suzi and Anna make red currant pastries for dessert.

Paprika is a powder made from the ground pods of the paprika plant. The red pods are dried before being ground. There are many different kinds of paprika, mixed in different ways, and all have names. *Félédes* is semi-sweet, and *erös* is hot and fiery. The paprika is kept fresh in the refrigerator.

On Sundays, if there are services with special music, the girls go with their mother to the Matthias Church, which is close to her office. Normally, though, they attend the Roman Catholic church near their house. Many young people go to church, because it is a place where they can meet friends.

Girls in Hungary follow their mother's religion and boys follow their father's. Dr. Szegedy-Maszák and Zoltán are Protestants. In many of the villages outside Budapest, if a church has a rooster on top of the spire it means it is Protestant, and if it has a sphere it is Roman Catholic.

On Sunday afternoons, Suzi and Anna sometimes ride the streetcar from their house to Moscow Square, where they catch a bus that takes them across a bridge to an island in the Danube. They rent a bicycle to pedal in the park on the island.

The girls love to ride in the park, but they can't afford to go very often. They pass a hot spring, one of many in Hungary. Its water contains natural minerals, which are a traditional cure for aches and pains.

In the park there is a large stage for concerts and folk dancing. The government keeps the ticket cost of cultural events down so most people can afford to go to them. The dances are often fast and exciting. Men leap high in the air and slap the sides of their boots.

Near the streetcar station there is a small market with fresh fruit, vegetables, and flowers. The larger stalls sell goods that are grown on government farms, called collectives, outside Budapest. Individuals are allowed to sell small amounts of produce from their own gardens.

The countryside in Hungary is fertile, except for the mountains. Grapes are grown on the sunny hillsides in the northeast, and the Great Plain has orchards and fields of wheat. Apples and apricots are plentiful in the summer, and yellow peppers almost spill onto the sidewalk. Bananas and oranges have to be imported from warmer climates, though, and they are expensive and difficult to find.

Anna and Suzi love to dress up in the old family costumes, which are hand-embroidered. People still wear traditional clothes in the country for special festivals and weddings, but in the cities people mainly put on these clothes to entertain tourists.

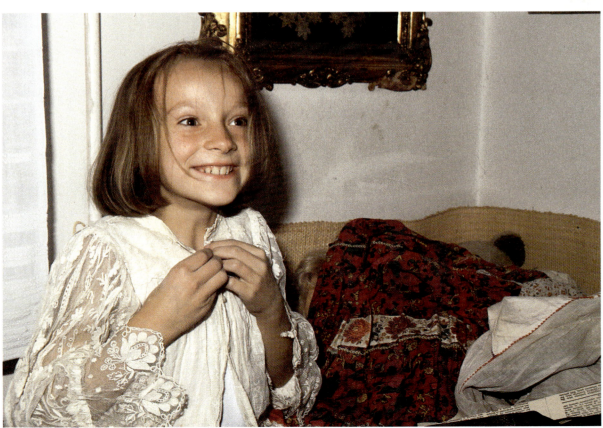

Hungarian horsemen also wear traditional costumes in horsemanship shows. Anna and Suzi hope to see a show someday. The riders gallop bareback across the plains rounding up long-horned cattle and herds of horses. It is easy to imagine that these men are descendants of the Magyars.

Dr. Szegedy-Maszák travels to work by streetcar. The university is in Pest, on the east bank of the Danube River. Pest is a mixture of tightly-packed industrial streets and wide, sweeping boulevards. Old, ornate buildings are interspersed with modern hotels. There are also offices and shops. When they need to buy clothes for school, Suzi and Anna travel into Pest with their father.

Sometimes their father has visitors at work, and he takes them to the town square for *kávé*, or espresso coffee, and cakes. In the summer people sit outside the cafes under brightly-colored umbrellas. The cafe in the picture is very old and well known in Budapest.

Anna and Suzi's uncle, Dr. Bánhegyi, lives in a village in the northeastern hills of Hungary. It takes about three hours to get to his village by car. The family goes to his house on August 20 to celebrate St. Stephen's Day, or Constitution Day, which is a national holiday. On that day in the year A.D. 1000, Stephen—who was later made a saint—was crowned the first king of Hungary. August 20 is also the time of the harvest, when the villages have new flour for baking bread.

Anna's mother provides the ingredients for *gulyás*, or goulash. This is a traditional Hungarian soup made from meat, carrots, onions, tomatoes, and paprika. Anna shapes dough into tiny dumplings to add to the stew before it is served.

In October the family helps pick grapes from Uncle Bánhegyi's vineyard. They crush them to make wine. They keep the wine in Uncle Bánhegyi's cellar at the bottom of the garden. The walls of the wine cellar are covered with a special mold which helps the wine ferment.

Glasses are raised for a toast, and the gulyás is served. The main course follows: stuffed pork, salad, vegetables, and fresh bread. For dessert, cake and watermelon are brought to the table with kávé.

The family returns to Budapest for a fireworks display in the evening. The houses of Parliament are brightly lit, and hundreds of people watch from the bridges as exploding patterns of light are reflected in the Danube.

The Hungarian Language

Magyar, or Hungarian, is spoken by only about 15 million people in the world, most of them in Hungary. Hungarian is unlike other languages in Eastern or Western Europe. Most European and North American languages, including English, stemmed from a common language centuries ago. The Hungarian language is related to Finnish, spoken mainly in Finland, and Estonian, spoken in part of the Soviet Union.

Hungarian Names and Words in This Book

Anna	AHN-nah
Bánhegyi	BAHN-hay-djee
Bundás	BOON-dosh
erös	AIR-uhsh
félédes	FAYL-ay-desh
gulyás	GOO-yahsh
kávé	KAH-vay
köpeny	KUH-pen-yuh
Magyar	MAH-djar
puli	POOH-lee
Szegedy-Maszák	SEH-geh-dee MA-sahk
Zsuzsa	ZHOO-zhah
Zoltán	ZOL-tahn

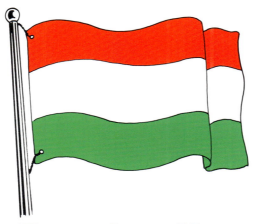

Facts about Hungary

Capital: Budapest

Language: Magyar (Hungarian)

Form of Money: forint

Area: 35,919 square miles
(93,030 square kilometers)
> Hungary is a little smaller than the state of Indiana.

Population: About 11 million people
> Hungary has about twice the population of Indiana.

NORTH
AMERICA

SOUTH
AMERICA

EUROPE

ASIA

Hungary

AFRICA

AUSTRALIA

31

Families the World Over

Some children in foreign countries live like you do. Others live very differently. In these books, you can meet children from all over the world. You'll learn about their games and schools, their families and friends, and what it's like to grow up in a faraway land.

Lerner Publications Company, 241 First Avenue North, Minneapolis, Minnesota 55401